The
POTATO
BOOK

J.C. NEWSHAM

with an introduction
by Kathy Clugston

BODLEIAN
LIBRARY
PUBLISHING

This book was first published in 1917, during the First World War.
It reflects the horticultural knowledge, views and attitudes of the period.

This edition published in 2024 by Bodleian Library Publishing,
Broad Street, Oxford OX1 3BG

www.bodleianshop.co.uk

ISBN 978 1 85124 623 6

All images, unless specified, © Bodleian Library, University of Oxford,
2024
Introduction © Kathy Clugston, 2024
This edition © Bodleian Library Publishing, University of Oxford, 2024

First published in 1917 by 'The Smallholder and Small Owner',
Covent Garden

Publisher: Samuel Fanous
Managing Editor: Susie Foster
Editor: Janet Phillips
Picture Editor: Leanda Shrimpton
Designed and typeset by Lucy Morton at illuminati in 11 on 15 Bulmer
Printed and bound in China by C&C Offset Printing Co., Ltd.
on 120 gsm Chinese Baijin Pure woodfree

British Library Catalogue in Publishing Data
A CIP record of this publication is available from the British Library

CONTENTS

INTRODUCTION

This is the perfect little book for the potato-lover in your life. In my case, coming from Northern Ireland, that's literally everyone I know. We are world-famous for our love of tatties. Many moons ago, as a sixteen-year-old, I spent a summer in France working as a *jeune fille au pair*. I had been quite good at French at school but had never actually met a French person and was horrified to find that how they spoke bore little resemblance to the deliberate diction of my Belfast teachers. On my first evening there, the whole family gathered for dinner to welcome me. I barely understood a word of what was being said until a bowl of steaming boiled potatoes was proffered.

'Les irlandais aiment les pommes de terre, non?' said the grandmother, as she dug in with the serving spoon.

'Oui,' I stammered nervously. 'J'adore les pommes de terre.'

A large spoonful landed on my plate followed by another, and another, until they formed a teetering potato mountain. A follow-up sentence along the lines of, 'Well, yeah, I mean I *like* potatoes but not that much…' was way beyond me, so I just smiled and nodded and ate them all up. From then on, at every single meal I was served my own supplementary dish of potatoes to add to those already on the plate. Fortunately, I was not sickened by the daily surfeit of spuds, just a bit thicker around the waist.

Ireland's history is intertwined with that of the potato. When the new vegetable discovery was brought to Europe from South America in the 1500s, its ugly and, many believed, poisonous tubers were treated with disdain by everyone except the Irish. They realized the plants would thrive in the temperate climate and soon saw the value of a crop that was nutritious and easy to grow, harvest and cook. Half an acre of land could feed a family for a year, including the animals. During the first wave of Irish emigrants to America in the early 1700s, a sack of seed potatoes was brought from Derry to New Hampshire, making it the first US state to cultivate them. Back home, everyone, rich or poor, ate potatoes at every meal; the poor ate little else. When the devastating potato blight hit in the mid-1840s, causing what became known as the Great Famine, a million people starved to death and at least another million fled the country. Most never returned, and they say Ireland's population has never truly recovered.

The country's love of the potato, though, remains undiminished. Even the Irish Lumper, the waxy, knobbly, somewhat tasteless variety on which the lower classes depended and which was all but wiped out, has been recultivated and sold as an heirloom variety. Like the Inuit with words for snow, so are the Irish blessed with dishes containing spuds. They are an essential component of the cuisine, north and south. A bowl of Irish stew, potato soup, boxty (potato pancakes), champ or colcannon can be washed down with a glass of poitín (a clear, unaged spirit that predates Irish whiskey). For breakfast, no Ulster Fry is complete without a potato farl or fadge.

When this book was first published in 1917, Britons were also getting their teeth into this particular delicacy as the wartime government energetically championed potatoes as a substitute for wheat, which was in short supply and needed for the troops. The newly established Ministry of Food sent officials all over the country extolling the virtues of potato bread. Advertisements containing recipes were placed in newspapers, and posters proclaimed 'Potatoes May Win the War!' Thus, J.C. Newsham's *The Potato Book* was well timed. Most of Newsham's horticultural works were aimed at the farmer or smallholder, with titles such as *Crops and Tillage* and *The Propagation and Pruning of Hardy Trees, Shrubs, and Miscellaneous Plants*, but this slim volume extended its scope to take in the amateur grower and help the patriotic citizen cultivate a Victory garden.

Much of the fun of reading a book that is more than a hundred years old is in noting how much or little has changed. These days, supermarket spud buyers not only miss out on the excitement of unearthing home-grown produce; they are limited to a small range of common varieties. Newsham is full of recommendations for potatoes with evocative names like Ashleaf Kidney, What's Wanted and The School Master, many of which have long since passed out of favour. Kerr's Pink, a floury variety widely available today, is described as 'a promising, new heavy-yielding sort'. He devotes a paragraph to growing earlies in pots – very relevant to today's urban grower – and would doubtless have approved of the yet-to-be-invented growbag.

Most of the potato questions we receive on *Gardeners' Question Time* concern disease, 'earthing up' (drawing up soil around the base of the plant as it grows) and 'chitting' (letting seed potatoes grow sprouts before planting). All of these topics are explored in the book; Newsham's detailed guide to constructing a wooden tray specifically for chitting rather knocks into a cocked hat our usual advice of using an old egg box. Newsham exhorts us to propagate, grow, store and eat potatoes with gusto and, if you are bewildered by the many ways you can cook them, offers us 'The Correct Method'.

The author would surely agree with his contemporary, the writer A.A. Milne, who wrote: 'What I say is that, if a fellow really likes potatoes, he must be a pretty decent sort of fellow.'[*]

KATHY CLUGSTON
Chair of *Gardeners' Question Time,* BBC Radio 4

---

[*] Writing at a time when 'man' was a generic term for 'human'. From 'Lunch' in *Not That It Matters*, 1919.

Chapter 1

WHAT WE OWE TO THE POTATO

Never before in the history of the world has this excellent vegetable been more worthy of the cultivator's attention. The great 'world war' has awakened not only Great Britain, but other countries, to the necessity for producing, as far as is possible, a food supply within its own boundaries, and none has greater necessity for this than England with an ever increasing population, that for so many centuries has so largely relied upon foreign enterprise for the supply of its markets.

In the potato we have a wonderful example of a wild plant being utilised as food for human consumption or for live stock. Nowhere in the vegetable kingdom has man's labour been crowned with such momentous results as in the development of the potato, not only as a food but also in the arts and manufactures.

EVERY DISH – POTATOES!

Towards the end of the eighteenth century a French savant, named Monsieur Parmentier, gave a banquet to celebrated men of the day, including Benjamin Franklin, and at which every dish consisted of potatoes cooked and dressed in a variety of different ways. It is also said that even the liquors drunk on this occasion were prepared from the potato. His idea in carrying out so novel a project was to familiarise the world with the great utility of the potato.

For many years Germany has been the best potato-growing country in the world. Potato cultivation, like all farming on a large scale in Germany, is based on an exact knowledge of the soil. This includes not only the elements it contains but its underlying strata, exposure, elevation and surroundings, whether shaded by adjacent woodlands or buildings, and especially its susceptibility to natural efficient drainage.

SECRET OF GERMAN SUCCESS

The secret of German pre-eminence in potato cultivation consists in the patient, careful, scientific preparation of the soil, not only for the restoration of its exhaustive fertility, but by mellowing, enriching and revivifying it by deep cultivation and the ploughing in of green manure crops which have taken up and digested the crude mineral fertilisation. Land thus prepared will yield three or even four crops of potatoes before their quality or quantity will begin to deteriorate, although the majority of growers exchange 'seed' with their neighbours.

As with apples, there are by far too many varieties of potatoes grown in this country. The Germans had before the war reduced their number of varieties to something like twenty standard sorts, as against some five hundred some thirty or so years previously.

There are some thousands of varieties in this country, while fifty at the most would be ample, including garden or non-commercial varieties.

As a nation we have not yet taken full advantage of the possibilities which the potato holds out, and which have been a great source of revenue to other countries.

WHAT THE POTATO CONTAINS

The composition of the potato is very simple as it roughly comprises 21 per cent of *starch* and 4 per cent fat and mineral matter, the remainder being water.

Now starch, although found plentifully and widely distributed throughout the vegetable kingdom, is a very valuable material, as it is quite easy for chemists to prepare a host of very useful materials from it; in fact, it would be difficult to find any industry in which starch products in one form or another are not very largely used. For example, starch may be readily fermented by yeast and then forms the spirit known as *alcohol*, and it is therefore largely used as a substitute for malt in the manufacture of beer and whisky. Moreover, the residue left after the spirit is distilled may be fed to live stock and in this way the nitrogenous matter and mineral salts are returned to the soil from which they had been

removed by the potatoes. The starch, on the other hand, consists of carbon, hydrogen and oxygen, substances which are obtained from the atmosphere, where they are present in inexhaustible quantities.

USE OF POTATO SPIRIT

The alcohol obtained from potato starch is of the greatest possible industrial value, whether it be in the manufacture of dyes from coal-tar, enamels, lacquers, varnishes, or as a solvent, as, for example, in the rubber industry. Again, the distilled potato spirit may even be used for lighting purposes or for motor power. Moreover, a by-product of alcohol known as *acetone* is very largely used in the manufacture of smokeless powder. Chloroform and ether are obtained from alcohol, while the majority of disinfectants also contain it.

Most of the macaroni, vermicelli and 'corn' flour is really made from potato starch, while sago more often than not is the artificial product of the same material instead of the 'pearled' flour obtained from the sago palm. Then the extent to which starch itself may be used seems limitless, for in addition to its utility for ordinary domestic purposes, the laundries use up enormous quantities and thousands of tons are consumed every year by the linen and cotton industries.

PROVIDES SUBSTITUTE FOR SUGAR

If the starch is simply boiled with an acid another valuable substance is produced, which is known as *dextrose*, glucose or starch sugar. This may be sold in the form of a syrup or in hard lumps, and for many purposes forms an excellent substitute for ordinary sugar. It is also used in the manufacture of paper and ink, and hundreds of tons of it are used for what the manufacturers call the improvement of honey, tobacco and confectionery.

Starch paste, made from boiling potato starch in water, which causes the starch grains to swell up and burst, is a gummy, whitish fluid, and this, if carefully heated so as not to char, forms what is known as *dextrine* or British gum, largely used for stiffening cotton goods, sizing paper, thickening colours in calico printing, making lozenges, adhesive stamps and labels, and for surgical bandages. Other gelatinous solutions of starch products are largely used for producing artificial silk, and for the production of celluloid.

To return to the uses of the raw potato itself. In addition to the more ordinary culinary uses, we have the manufacture of potato bread, made by mixing boiled potatoes with flour. Potatoes may also be subjected to desiccation, or very thorough drying, which will allow them to be kept for an indefinite time in highly concentrated form as potato 'flakes'. This process forms a huge industry on the Continent, the resulting dried flakes forming a nourishing heat and work producing food for both man and beast.

Chapter 2

WHERE THE
POTATO THRIVES

History proverbially repeats itself, and we read of the distress which prevailed in England during the early part of the nineteenth century, when the Corn Laws were in full force, and flour rose in price to close on 30*s*. per bushel, and bread riots were experienced. Again, we are now at the beginning of the twentieth century confronted with high prices for wheat and a corresponding increase in the price of potatoes. Had conditions been such that we were still more restricted to our home food supplies, it requires very little imagination to realise what the end would have been.

Now as to the question as to whether the cultivation of wheat or of potatoes should have the preference. There can be no doubt that from a given area of land a greater amount of nutritious food is grown in the form of potatoes than in the form of wheat, assuming that average yields of each crop are forthcoming. We must look to our agricultural chemists for confirmation of these facts, and without referring to statistics it will suffice to say that if a piece of ground sown to wheat will maintain one man, then the same ground planted with potatoes would maintain four men in so far as the nutritive powers of these crops depend upon the starch, sugar and gum they contain.

WHY POTATOES MAKE FINE FOODS

In the nourishment of the human body, protein or albuminoids, as well as carbohydrates (starch and sugar), are essential. While the carbohydrates, or foods lacking in nitrogen, combine with the oxygen in the lungs to give warmth, the nitrogenous ingredients nourish the muscular system, thereby enabling man to perform his labours. It is the combination of these nutritive properties in natural foods therefore that is so important, and that cannot be produced so cheaply from any other source. The nitrogenous portion, whether it be in foods or manures, is always the most costly to purchase. The potato is a very valuable food, as it contains hydrogen, carbon, nitrogen, phosphorus, sulphur, iron and lime, all elements required for building up and maintaining the body in health by replacing worn-out tissue.

There is little time in these days for studying the history of plants, however interesting and fascinating that history may be. I need only say, therefore, that the potato (*Solanum tuberosum*) is a native of South America, where it grows wild over a large tract of country on the western side of the southern states, especially in Peru, Ecuador and Chile. In its natural state the plant grows very luxuriantly, the stems often reaching a height of 6 or 7 feet in swampy situations, and where they may often become recumbent or trailing.

The tubers are variable in colour and may be red, white or yellow-skinned blotched with red; they are small and irregular in shape, and very sparingly produced, the inclination of the plant being to develop its tubers above rather than below the surface of the soil.

The tubers of the cultivated potato vary greatly in size, form and colour, and for convenience they are divided into rounded forms and long forms or 'kidneys', and there are of course intermediate varieties. The colour of the skin, that is yellowish, brown or purple, furnishes distinctions, as also does the yellow or white colour of the flesh. The colour of the eyes, and their prominence or depth, are relatively very constant characteristics.

HOW ITS CULTURE SPREAD

The potato was grown on the continent of Europe before its introduction into England, having been introduced into Spain from Quito by the Spaniards in the earlier part of the sixteenth century. A Vienna botanist, named Clusium, is credited with having obtained it from Mons in Belgium in 1598, and later, when introduced into Germany, its culture spread by leaps and bounds, and our enemies were not slow in appreciating its many merits.

A great deal more might be said in regard to the introduction of the plant into this country, but briefly there appears little doubt that tubers were first brought to Ireland by Sir Frances Drake on his return voyage from South America, and presented to Sir Walter Raleigh in 1586.

Sir Walter Raleigh, therefore, really had nothing to do with the introduction of the potato, although he may have been the first man to bring its cultivation under the notice of people in this country.

Prior to 1597 the potato had not received a name, and it was Gerard who first gave it the name of 'potato', when publishing his *Herbal*, on account of its resemblance to the sweet potato (*Ipomoea batatas*).

GROWN FROM POLE TO POLE!

It is interesting to note that the potato has the widest geographical range of any cultivated plant, being found from the southern extremity of Africa to Labrador, Iceland and Lapland. It is also one of the most accommodating plants as regards soil conditions and general cultivation. It will thrive in bog or peat soil of which 70 to 75 per cent is organic matter, to a clay soil with only 2 to 5 per cent organic matter, with fairly satisfactory results if the soil be properly treated as regards tillage.

Tillage is the first principle of good culture. Deep ploughing or digging according to the character of the soil so as to expose the mass to the weathering effects of climate, accompanied by judicious manuring, are essentials towards success.

A friable or 'crumbly' soil is the ideal one for potatoes, and the deeper it is the better. Water-logged soils on which the plough or spade turns up a shining furrow or 'spit', or where the tillage implement touches water, can never grow potatoes satisfactorily. Above all things thorough drainage is essential.

CULTIVATION ON BRITISH SOILS

For all classes of soils the cultivation in the autumn is alike, and at this season the land should be well tilled to destroy weeds and to get it into a friable condition, after which it should be ploughed up deeply for the winter.

On the sandstone soils of Scotland, and in some parts of England which are best adapted for potatoes, cross-ploughing can be done with advantage in the spring, or in February, as it can also on the peaty land of Lincolnshire and on the good red soils of that county.

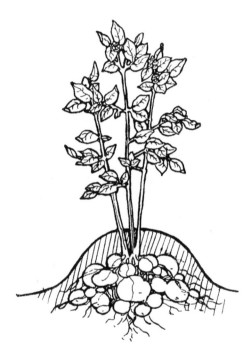

GOOD SUBSOIL AND FREE DRAINAGE

In a good subsoil the roots and stolons, or growths, have every opportunity of spreading, and the tubers develop under the soil.

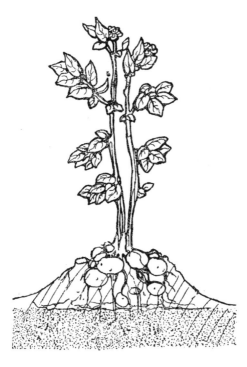

BAD SUBSOIL AND POOR DRAINAGE

On bad and shallow soils root growth is
restricted, and the tubers are inclined to form
high up the stem above the surface level.

On clay soils, such as those of the Weald of Sussex, ploughing in spring is often somewhat hazardous, unless the land is in an exceptionally dry condition. When it turns up wet and 'livery' there is great difficulty in working it into the mass of fine mould essential to the complete success of the potato crop. The writer had the privilege of serving on the committee of the National Potato Society, and has always regretted that this useful society was allowed to become defunct, as it was capable of performing work of national importance in connection with the potato industry of this country.

WILL THERE BE A POTATO 'BOOM'?

Never before since the days of the 'potato boom' has there been so much stir amongst potato growers. The great potato boom of 1903 was in peace time, and the much discussed 'El Dorado' then frequently changed hands at £100 per lb, while many other new varieties made exorbitant prices.

Now we are confronted with quite a different kind of boom, namely a natural desire to supplement the nation's food supply, when everyone is expected to do their very utmost to increase their area under potatoes.

Although there is no particular need to propagate potatoes from cuttings, or to adopt other means of equally rapid increase, the existing stock of seed in the country should be grown to the best advantage.

Chapter 3

HOW TO PROPAGATE
THE POTATO

The propagation of the potato is best left in the hands of the experts or those nurserymen who specialise in potato cultivation. In raising new and improved varieties of potatoes from seed considerable patience as well as care is involved. Plants that have been improved by crossing have a tendency to degenerate, or revert to their original state, and the potato possesses this tendency to a greater degree than most plants. Therefore little good results from the indiscriminate gathering and sowing of seed of varieties that have not been judiciously crossed, or hybridised, as tests have demonstrated that not one seed in a hundred thousand will produce an improved variety.

Hybridisation, or, to be more correct, cross-breeding, is in itself a very simple process. Having selected the varieties to be crossed, the seed-bearing parent first calls for attention. When the flower buds appear they should all be removed, except those which are to be impregnated, and when the flowers open the stamens should be removed with a pair of tweezers or sharp-pointed scissors, taking care not to damage the pistil or female organ of the plant.

WHEN FERTILISATION OCCURS

Tie the truss of bloom to a stake and cover over with a piece of gauze to guard against premature fertilisation by insect agency. In two days or so after the flowers have been expanded, and provided the weather is favourable, they will be in a fit state for the reception of pollen grains. A flower is taken from the plant which is to be the 'male parent' of the future seedlings, and the pollen from its anthers carefully applied to the pistil of the plant that is to be the 'female parent' or seed-bearer. Fertilisation will usually take place within a few hours after the

19

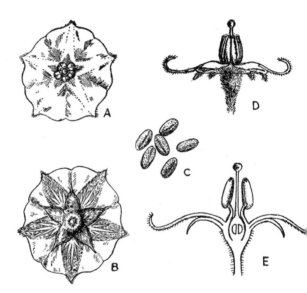

THE POTATO FLOWER

A Upper surface of flower.
B Under surface. C Seed.
D & E Sections of flower showing stamen,
ovary style and stigma

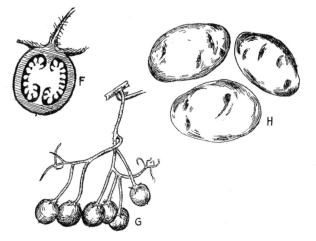

**POTATO FRUIT OR TRUE SEED
('POTATO PLUM')**

F Transverse section of ovary.
G Fruit. H Tubers.

pollen has been applied, after which the gauze may be removed.

The berries when ripe should be opened and the seeds removed. In cleaning the seeds free from pulp I have found it advisable, as in the case of tomatoes, to allow the pulp containing the seed to ferment slightly in water, after which the seeds can be more readily separated out and washed. Dry the seeds thoroughly after washing, and store away in paper packets until February or whenever required for sowing. As each berry contains anything from 100 to 300 seeds, there is no necessity to fertilise more than one flower unless the raising of seedlings is undertaken on a large scale.

Rarely do the seedlings represent the two parents in a perfectly intermediate degree; the general habit is usually that of the female parent or seed-bearing plant, while the colour of the flower and tuber usually resembles the male plant.

No definite principle can however be laid down, because, as a rule, the plant that possesses the strongest habit and constitution should be made the seed-bearing plant.

SOME VARIETIES NEVER FLOWER

Some varieties of potatoes never flower, while others are very shy of flowering and seldom produce seed-balls (potato plums). In some cases the young tubers should be removed from the 'root' as soon as formed, so that the whole energy of the plant may be concentrated towards perfecting its fruit. By this means seed may often be obtained from varieties which under ordinary cultivation seldom mature their seed. As the method of saving and sowing the seed is similar to that practised in the case of most half-hardy annuals I need hardly occupy space in describing it.

The tubers produced from the seedlings in the first year are naturally very small, the largest rarely being bigger than a pullet's egg, while the average are nearer the size of hazel nuts. It is evident, therefore, that no reliable selection can be made until the second year of growth. This means that a fairly large area of ground must be preserved for planting out the seedling tubers. At the end of the second year a definite selection may be made, and should it happen that a promising seedling is obtained, the more rapidly this can be propagated in order to obtain a stock the better.

WHAT ABOUT CUTTINGS?

This brings us to the question of cuttings. Potatoes may be quickly reproduced by cuttings. By way of example, we may take one pound of potatoes, consisting of four tubers, averaging twelve eyes each, making a total of forty-eight eyes. The 'eye' of the potato consists of several buds, anything up to six, and when planted in the ordinary way only one, or at the most two, buds start into growth, the others remaining dormant. If, however, each eye is subdivided into as many sets as there are buds, every germ is brought into active growth.

The propagation would be very similar to that practised with dahlias. The sets being small they must be carefully planted, say early in February, in three- or four-inch pots, using a light loamy compost, and placed in a warm frame at a temperature of 50°F or just sufficient to encourage growth. Give just sufficient water to stimulate root action.

When the shoots have attained a height of about six inches their tops should be cut off and inserted in single pots and placed in a hot-bed with a bottom heat of about 65 to 70°F, when the cuttings will readily root. If plunged in a bed of cocoa-nut fibre so much the better.

When these cuttings have attained a reasonable height, say two and a half inches, their tops in turn are removed, as also are the side or lateral growths of the original plants. This process of increasing the number of plants may be continued until May or until such time as it becomes necessary to harden off and plant out in the open ground.

Unlike wheat and other cereals, equally essential as food, potatoes may be successfully grown in the smallest garden whether it be in town or country. I would go so far as to say that, if they only would take the trouble, most householders with gardens of a fair size could actually become self-supporting so far as this vegetable is concerned.

At any rate, one thing is certain. Everybody who possibly can ought to grow potatoes even if it be only a few pounds.

Chapter 4

IMPORTANCE
OF GOOD SEED

The first thing that the grower has to consider is the quality of the potatoes he is going to plant. Don't plant rubbish. And don't think that because your neighbour has given you a few seed potatoes he has bestowed a blessing upon you. Oh, no! While much of the so-called 'seed' is quite wholesome food for pigs, it is worthless for planting purposes.

Bear in mind, too, that however good a new variety of potato may be when it is first introduced it gradually deteriorates or loses its original strength and quality. It may, however, be kept in a fairly good condition for many years, provided that a very careful selection is made each year of the tubers it is intended to plant. If you purchased new 'seed' or stock last year, hold on to it, as every tuber will be required for planting. It is a good plan to import new 'seed' from Scotland each season so as to be in a position to sell a portion of the produce each year. Once grown, Scotch 'seed' not unusually gives a heavier yield than that newly imported.

WHAT ABOUT IRISH 'SEED'?

Excellent results also attend the planting of Irish 'seed', and in the important trials carried out by Messrs Sutton & Sons at Reading some years ago there was little to choose between the Scotch and Irish 'seed'. In the second year, however, I have found the Scotch seed to yield heavier, and this assumption is based on some ten or more years' continuous experiments.

Whatever you do, don't wait until planting time before you consider what quantity of potatoes you will grow. In the southern districts of England, where the climate is dry and warm, a change of 'seed' from Scotland or from Ireland is desirable every year, but in the northern or cooler parts a change every second or third year is usually sufficient.

NEIGHBOURS SHOULD EXCHANGE SEED

A very good plan is for cottage gardeners and allotment holders to exchange 'seed' one with the other, provided that their soils are opposite in character. For example, the man with the heavy retentive soil should exchange with the man whose soil is light and sandy, and vice versa.

The same variety of potato may be grown on the same farm for ten or more years with excellent results, merely by planting alternately in light and heavy soils.

There is a vast difference in the constitution of potatoes, so far as their capacity of being grown under the same soil and climate conditions is concerned. Magnum-bonum was an exception in this respect, and was known to retain its vigour for something like twenty years, when cultivated under similar climatic and soil conditions, but this is quite an exception to the rule.

SOILS OFTEN BECOME 'SICK'

If potatoes are grown in the same soil year after year, that particular soil gets, as it were, sick of potatoes, and although the exact reason may not be easy to explain, it can quite well be imagined. 'A change of soil is as good as a change of seed.' This remark, although applying to cereals and the majority of other crops, applies with more truth to potatoes than to any other plant.

Quite the most important thing the grower of potatoes has to consider each season is the selection of suitable varieties for planting. In my opinion it is a mistake to stick to the same sorts year after year, although on the other hand I don't recommend anyone to jump, as it were, at new varieties, about the qualities of which little or nothing is known.

Somebody must, of course, give a trial to the more recently introduced varieties, but that to my mind is best left to the expert. If the beginner cares to accept the risk, let him experiment with a few pounds of 'seed' to begin with. Then he will have gained valuable knowledge for future occasions, and without having incurred any serious pecuniary loss.

STICK TO APPROVED VARIETIES

Ordinarily, however, the small grower will be well advised to confine himself to a few approved varieties as follows:

EARLY May Queen, Sharpe's Express, Sharpe's Victor, Improved Ashleaf and Early Midlothian.

MID-SEASON British Queen, Great Scot and Duke of York.

LATE Factor, Up-to-Date, King Edward and Arran Chief.

These few varieties are merely given for guidance, and may not hold good for many years.

Chapter 5

ALL ABOUT DISEASE-RESISTING VARIETIES

No good purpose would be served by giving here a long list of first and second earlies or of mid-season or late varieties, because, after all, what the average grower wants is to secure potatoes as early in the season as he can. Moreover, readers can always see lists of these in any trade catalogue. At the same time I would just like to mention a few special varieties, which may be less familiar, and all of which resist the dreaded wart disease.

As a first early, Sutton's A1 may be recommended, the tubers of which are round, of medium size with a white skin and yellow flesh. As with many early potatoes, however, the yield is light and the proportion of small tubers large.

Findlay's Conquest is a reliable second early. The tubers are round, of large size, with a thin white skin and white flesh. The yield moreover is good.

As the tubers are produced near the surface of the soil, and close up to the stem, the plants require to be earthed up high.

GOOD SECOND EARLIES

Other second earlies are Snowball, King Albert, The Schoolmaster, King George and Great Scot. The last-named is well suited for growing in poor soils. Though its quality is good, however, very large tubers are apt to be hollow, a defect which also applies to Arran Chief.

In many districts, Great Scot is considered the best second early, resistant to wart disease, for field cultivation.

Among late varieties we have Sutton's Abundance and Leinster Wonder, both of which appear fairly resistant to common potato disease.

There are also others like Southampton Wonder, which resembles Great Scot, and Culdees Castle and Provost, which resemble Abundance, to say nothing of Irish Queen, Shamrock Laird, Flour-ball, What's

Wanted and White City. Any of the above, moreover, have been very carefully tested.

'WARE WART DISEASE

It is well to remember that it is illegal to plant potatoes on land infested with wart disease, except under a licence granted by a Board of Agriculture Inspector. In any case, the following varieties are highly susceptible to the disease, and must not be planted on infected land: Early Puritan, Epicure, Early Midlothian, British Queen, Duke of York, Sharpe's Express, Sharpe's Victor, Arran Chief, Sir John Llewellyn, Evergood, Cora, Cigarette, King Edward VII, Up-to-Date, Dalhousie, Duchess of Cornwall, Factor and Prolific.

We have seen excellent samples of some of the newer introductions like the New Early Red Kidney, and New Success, of second earlies like The Ally, Irish Queen and Scottish Standard, and in main crops of the Late New Kidney, Summit and Vitality. Kerr's Pink is another promising new heavy-yielding sort, while the excellent new varieties introduced by potato growers of repute are always worthy of consideration.

WHAT TO LOOK FOR

In the selection of tubers for seed considerable care must be exercised, as the same variety of potato will vary so much in constitution according to how it has been grown. Vitality and strength of constitution are what we want to look for in our 'seed' tubers. To obtain these qualities we must secure tubers which have not been allowed to become too ripe or over-matured, as is the case when they are grown on light, warm soils in the South of England.

When potatoes become too ripe they contain a large amount of starch. True, the over-ripe potato, with its thick net-veined skin, will usually cook well and be floury, but the good cooking potato is just what must be avoided for planting.

The potato which when cooked presents a 'waxy' condition, and which few people relish, is the one with plenty of constitution and vigour. It contains less starch and more nitrogen in its composition. In order to obtain this waxiness potatoes must be raised while the haulm is still green, and this is what large growers who specialise in seed potatoes always do.

If the grower of culinary potatoes wishes to check this waxy or watery texture, he can do so by

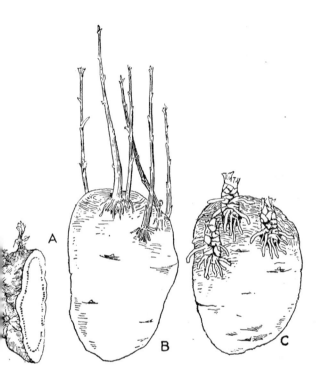

TUBERS

A Always cut seed tubers from the crown downwards.
B Tubers with long, thin and blanched growths
are inferior as seed.
C When exposed to light, air and low temperature
the growths are short.

increasing the amount of phosphates and potash in the soil and reducing the nitrogen content.

THE ART OF STORING

Having decided upon the quality and quantity of seed required for the season's planting, we must next consider how best to treat and store during winter till the time of planting.

In my opinion tubers required for early planting are best kept in baskets or boxes. If properly constructed trays are available so much the better, for these, while admitting of being stacked one on top of the other, also ensure a free circulation of air and light, both essential conditions which are not so easily obtainable with ordinary boxes.

The increased cost of foreign timber has in many cases necessitated substitutes being found. Herring boxes are excellent and can be purchased very cheaply. The only drawback is that they smell strongly of the fish, so that they are somewhat objectionable in the house; but where there is an outhouse or shed I advise their use instead of trays or chitting boxes.

PACKING IN BOXES

The packing of the tubers for sprouting in the boxes can best be performed when the box is slightly tilted. Also when placing the tubers in the boxes see that the growing ends of the tubers – that is, the ends where 'eyes' are prominent – are placed uppermost, unless it is preferred to place two or more layers in each box.

Now regarding the kind of sets to choose. Some people think that the 'tare or chats' (pig potatoes), or refuse, are good enough, but I do not agree with them. On the contrary the best, and not the worst, ought to be used. Sets or seed should be of even size, two to three ounces in weight. To plant a larger set is waste, and smaller ones scarcely give satisfaction.

If any very large tubers are planted, they should be divided or cut so that each portion has at least two sprouts. As these large potatoes have different degrees of size and development, no definite rule can be laid down as regards cutting, except to say that the cuttings should proceed from the crown downwards. This secures for each set a good proportion of vigorous sprouts.

WON'T STAND CUTTING

There are just a few potatoes that will not stand cutting, and one is Arran Chief. I have tried dressing the cut surface with a drying medium but without effect. If cut tubers of this variety are planted blanks in the rows must be expected.

A common mistake which many make is to cut the tubers at the time of setting. Now newly cut sets are very liable to rot or to be destroyed by insects, to say nothing of the fact that a fresh cut or wound causes bleeding and renders the exposed surface an easy prey to all kinds of insect pests and fungoid diseases. The risk is reduced, however, if the sets are cut some days before planting, so that the wound may become healed by exposure to the air. A little powdered charcoal, flowers of sulphur or slaked lime sprinkled over a freshly cut surface will soon form a new skin.

CUT TUBERS GROW QUICKLY

I have observed that this cutting of the tubers greatly encourages the quick growth of the plant, a point of great importance. Further, it will be found that half of a large tuber has a hereditary vigour greater than that of a whole small tuber, and if the number of tubers obtained is no more their size is greater.

If the shoots on sprouted tubers have become drawn up, weak and elongated through being stored in a dark cellar, it may be better to rub off the shoots so as to encourage a second crop of more sturdy sprouts.

Chapter 6

THE ART OF
PLANTING POTATOES

Potatoes which have thrown out long shoots in a cellar should not be used for planting. My heaviest yields are always obtained from sets which have been sprouted in the open air in a warm but airy spot until the shoots have reached a length of about one inch. These rudimentary shoots grow more quickly, become thicker, give finer leaves, and are less likely to be broken; also the germs are strong enough to stand the risk of planting and other dangers.

Other advantages of forcing vegetation in this manner in the open air are that much time is saved, especially in bad weather, or if the ground is not prepared, the yield will be much increased both in number of tubers or gross weight, and the produce will be much richer in starch and cook better.

It is not going too far to say that thousands of tons of sound potatoes are lost every year owing to careless clamping or storing on the ground. Perhaps the greatest evil is wrought by allowing them to become heated in the clamps, as when this takes place the potatoes may appear reasonably sound upon external examination, but when placed in the ground they make little or no growth.

It is not as though there were any great difficulty about the clamping or pitting of potatoes. Ordinary care is needed, that is all. Clamps should not be more than 5 foot wide for tubers showing signs of disease, as against 8 foot wide for large sound tubers.

THE DISTANCE APART

The distance apart at which to plant potatoes often appears confusing to the beginner. In spacing out the distance for any plant it is well to picture in one's mind the size of the plant when fully developed. Varieties of potatoes vary considerably in their habits of growth and wealth of foliage. Early potatoes will occupy little space, whereas the main crop varieties cover a fairly large area. In all cases allow plenty of room between the rows, and for the strong growers thirty inches is not too much, the tubers being planted about fourteen inches apart in the rows.

For early varieties twenty inches apart between the rows and ten inches from plant to plant may be regarded as average distances. Where space is limited it is an excellent plan on good ground to plant early and late varieties in alternate rows two and a half feet apart. Early varieties such as Ashleaf are ready for lifting by the time the late sorts commence to throw out their stolons or runners on which the young tubers are formed. The early varieties can thus be lifted without injury to their neighbours. The soil in which they have grown will serve for earthing purposes for the late kinds, while the greater space will allow room for the mass of foliage which strong kinds usually produce.

Each grower must use his own judgment as regards spacing, as the quality of the 'seed', depth and fertility of the soil are all important factors to be considered.

HINTS ABOUT DEPTH

The depth at which to plant potatoes is another important matter. Early potatoes are all the better for being placed reasonably deep in good friable soils. The value of deep planting is that the plants are not so easily attacked by frost, and even though the tops of the plant suffer check there is usually enough stem below ground to guarantee a speedy recovery. Main crop varieties need not be planted so deep, although it must be remembered that some varieties of potatoes have a tendency to develop tubers much higher up the stem than others, and this must be taken into consideration when planting.

I have planted early potatoes as deep as eight inches, but this can only be done when the soil is deep and open, as for example in those garden soils which have been systematically trenched for years, and which, if not naturally light and porous, have been made so by the application of well decomposed farmyard manure or leaf mould. Usually five inches is a fair depth at which to plant early potatoes, and three to four inches for main-crop varieties. In field cultivation they should be deep enough to prevent the tines of the harrows or drags bringing them to the surface when working down the surface after planting. There is no more pleasing sight than to see the rows of potatoes sprouting regularly over the ground with no spaces to indicate that tubers have failed to do their duty.

THE AFTER-CULTIVATION

The after-cultivation of the crop is neither laborious nor difficult. Whether earthed up with the plough or by hand the soil between the drills should be loose and open. If it is not so, then the sooner the grubber, horse-hoe or mattock is worked between the rows to loosen the surface the better, and the operation should be repeated as frequently as possible.

Tubers obliged to develop in stiff retentive soils can never do so to advantage; in fact, they become any shape but round or oval, thus indicating that the soil pressure to which they are subjected prevents their free development. No! If potatoes are to attain to a fair average size the soil in which they grow must be mellow and porous; if fine, sweet and rich without being rank, and on a fairly dry bottom so much the better. I always like to work the drills down and put them up again twice before the potatoes are through the ground, using the semi-circular harrows or grubber according to the texture of the soil.

Do not allow the plants to topple over before earthing up is commenced, especially in the case of early varieties. The more gradually the earthing process is performed the better, and two or even three earthings-up during the growing season, or before the foliage renders this operation no longer practicable, are to be preferred to the more drastic process of giving only one earthing-up. If this important work is properly performed there would be no need for any hand-weeding of the crop in its later stages of growth.

THE 'LAZY-BED' SYSTEM

Another method of cultivation is that known as the lazy-bed system, largely practised in Ireland. In this case the ground is marked off into beds 4 ft or 5 ft broad, between which are trenches 1½ ft to 2 ft wide. A dressing of dung is spread over the beds, and the potatoes are planted on the surface. Earth from the trenches is laid over the dung to a depth of 3 or 4 in., and as the size of the plants increases more earth is laid over them. An advantage of this method is that the trenches act as drains, while if their position is moved each year the land will be thoroughly trenched to a good depth.

WHEN THE SOIL IS HEAVY

Where the soil is heavy the thing to do is to manure it freely during autumn or early winter with farmyard manure, digging or ploughing it in, and leave the soil ridged or roughed up, to be weathered by frost and wind. Then in the spring it will work or break down in a fine powdery condition. A second ploughing or digging on a dry day will still further improve the texture of the soil and ensure a good tilth at planting time.

The next best manure to 'farmyard' may be called 'common' manure. Where a pig, goats, fowls or even rabbits are kept the common manure heaps will be very like farmyard manure. Even without these the common heap may be converted into excellent plant food for potatoes. Old cabbage stumps and leaves, and other waste vegetable produce, also ditch scourings, road scrapings, closet refuse, wood ashes,

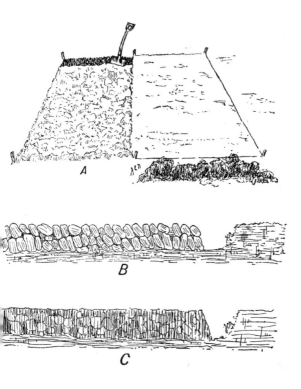

TRENCHING

In trenching or deepening soil there is no need to wheel
the contents of the first trench to the end of the ground.
Divide the ground into convenient widths, which will
admit of the soil being placed with the spade as shown
in A. As the work proceeds, the last open trench on the
plot will be ready to receive the first section removed.
Leave the surface rough as shown in B, and not as in C.

leaves, and such-like if well mixed and frequently turned and applied to the soil in autumn or early spring will greatly increase the yield; autumn application is, of course, preferable to spring. Many people say that coal ashes produce scab in potatoes. Cinders and coal dust certainly do so, but I have obtained excellent quality tubers when finely sifted coal ash has been incorporated with ordinary garden soil.

PLOUGHING IN THE SEED

The 'seed' tubers may be planted by ploughing them in with an ordinary plough, or, better still, a ridging plough to open the furrows, or they may be dibbled in. In gardens I much prefer to dig in the tubers, or, in other words, to plant them as the operation of spring digging or forking over the ground proceeds. In this way the ground does not get trodden and the tubers have every chance to develop their growth freely. The dibber may be used on light soils, as here a little pressure or consolidation of the soil does no harm.

On lighter soils, too, I believe in placing well-decayed manure in the furrows at the time of planting, but on good loamy soil the manure is of more service to the plant when spread on the surface and ploughed in, thus ensuring a more even distribution. It is all very well to say that if the ground has been well manured for a previous crop, like winter greens, then there is no need to manure again for potatoes. This may be true in the case of early potatoes to a certain extent, but to obtain heavy yields of either early or late potatoes I find it necessary to manure heavily every time. Also, it is well to remember that 10 tons of potatoes will extract the following manurial ingredients from the soil: 78 lb nitrogen, 80 lb phosphate and 128 lb potash.

My experience is that a mixture of farmyard manure and artificials is to be preferred to the use of either by itself. The amount of seed required will average 15 cwt per acre or 10 lb per rod, according to its size and the distance apart at which it is planted.

TIPS ABOUT MANURES

I have invariably obtained the heaviest yields of both early and late potatoes from the following manurial dressings:

Twenty tons per acre or 14 cwt per rod of well-decayed farmyard manure applied on heavy soils in autumn and on light soils in spring, accompanied in the spring by 2 cwt per acre or 1½ lb per rod of sulphate of ammonia and 5 cwt per acre or 3½ lb per rod of mineral superphosphate mixed together and broadcasted in the drills at planting time.

Five cwt per acre of kainit or 1½ cwt of sulphate of potash would be a useful addition to any potato soil, but it is useless to talk about a potash manure when there is little or none available or when what is available is prohibitive in price. That potatoes respond to potash, however, there can be no doubt, and a liberal application of this constituent not only gives a much increased yield, but results in a potato of high cooking quality due to increased starch formation.

A SUBSTITUTE FOR POTASH

As a substitute for potash I suggest the use of dry wood ashes when obtainable.

A good dusting of dry wood ashes in the drills will assist in producing clear-skinned tubers, a point to be noted by exhibitors.

Fresh soot is also a good manure for potatoes, applied at the rate of from twenty to thirty bushels per acre or 5 lb per rod at planting time, while gypsum and common salt are very beneficial in the lighter soils, using 3 cwt of the former and 2 cwt of the latter per acre.

Excellent crops of potatoes are grown in soils deficient in lime, and the potato is one of very few cultivated plants that grow well in slightly sour or acid soils. On peaty soils and bogs containing a large excess of organic matter and no lime in their composition, lime is undoubtedly essential. A too free use of lime will, however, often account for scab in potatoes.

HOW TO CROP DERELICT LAND

There is every prospect of large areas of old pasture ground being broken up for potatoes. On all newly broken-up soils potatoes grow with considerable vigour and a fairly heavy yield may be expected.

When old woods and coppices are grubbed up or old heath or bog land is reclaimed potatoes are usually the first crop to be grown. When oats or any other cereal crop is grown for the first time on virgin soil an excessive yield of straw is produced and little or no grain; so with the potato, an excess of haulm is often produced with little or no tubers on the lower portion of the stem, the cause of this rankness of growth being due to excess of nitrogen owing to the large amount of decaying organic matter present.

Where an old pasture or ley is to be broken up, it is best to disc it well with a disc cultivator, then plough it deeply. This admits of the turf rotting during the winter. Cross-plough again in the early spring, and work well with the cultivator and heavy drags during the drying days of March and April. Finally open the furrows with a boulting plough in readiness for planting. Where large tracts of old pasture are to be broken up for allotments, there is no more effective method of bringing them under cultivation.

Raftering is a process of dealing with old leys which might be more widely practised than it is at the present time. The process consists in turning over a shallow furrow on to an unploughed surface, producing a sandwiching effect on the grass, which is thus smothered. It is necessary for the rafters to remain in position a few weeks, after which it will be possible to completely work the soil and clean it.

Chapter 7

HOW TO RAISE
EARLY POTATOES

There are few vegetables more generally appreciated than new potatoes, and few find a more ready sale in our markets. In favourable districts no vegetable crop pays better for early growing, but in order to secure the best results it is not only necessary for the land to be fertile and the climate suitable to the growth of the plants, but especial care must be taken as regards cultural methods.

Many people have an idea that early potatoes can only be grown successfully in the southern counties, but this is not the case, as large areas are grown in the southern and western counties of Scotland, and in districts like Clonakilty in Ireland. The Ayrshire coast, warmed as it is by the Gulf Stream, is admirably adapted for early potato growing.

Turning to small cultivators, such as allotment-holders or even to private growers in small gardens, warm borders or sheltered corners are often obtainable. Early sprouted potatoes are often fit for planting in January in such positions, and if afforded a little protection the crop may be lifted very early, thus ensuring very high prices. In these situations it is preferable to plant on the flat, and this admits of a row of radishes, lettuces or other early maturing crop being planted between the rows, and these crops will be removed before the potatoes are ready for earthing up.

CULTURE UNDER GLASS

Very early crops of potatoes are sometimes obtained under glass, planted out in the borders of large tomato or similar types of houses, while in some instances they are grown in boxes or pots, and often in frames. In the latter case, well-decayed manure, leaf-mould or other fermenting material supplies the necessary heat.

The pits or frames are filled to within a foot or so of the glass with the fermenting compost, over which is placed about six inches of rich, light loamy soil. The sprouting 'sets' are planted in rows fifteen inches apart and about a foot apart in the rows. Never plant until the temperature of the bed has fallen below 70°F, otherwise the sets will be injured by scalding and will fail to grow. When the shoots are about six inches to eight inches in height commence to earth up by adding new soil, as if this is not done the young tubers which push up to the surface will become discoloured and unfit for use.

A little guano should be added to the soil at the time of planting, also wood ashes if available, as it is during the early stages of growth that the plants require nourishing. Also they do not remain long in the soil, as with careful treatment potatoes fit for market will be obtainable in April. An excess of nitrogen must be avoided, and if a concentrated form of potash like kainit or sulphate of potash is obtainable, give 2½ oz of the former or 1 oz of the latter per square yard.

HAVE YOU TRIED POT CULTURE?

Pot culture is quite simple wherever shelves are available in heated greenhouses or on stages not too far removed from the light. The very earliest sorts, like Ashleaf Kidney, can be best grown by means of pots, for which two particular sizes, '32' and '24', are most suitable, or margarine boxes will prove equally suitable. The '32' pots should receive one tuber each, and the '24' pots three tubers.

Commence planting in December and during the two subsequent months. It is an advantage to just start the plants in a cool frame, as the tubers commence growing more readily when transferred to a warm structure. Afterwards treat as advised for frame culture; that is, do not fill the pot too full of soil but leave sufficient room for earthing up with mould at a later stage.

Large consignments of potatoes come from the Canary Islands, also from Jersey and Guernsey, where the climate is exceptionally favourable to the growth of early potatoes, as here it is very seldom that frost injures the young growth.

The Canary Island potatoes are the first to arrive in England, followed by the Jerseys. These are followed by the Cornish, and then come the Ayrshire (Scotch) potatoes. The southern crops then follow and are soon used up, when later we have large bulks coming from the Dunbar districts in the east into our markets, and from Fifeshire and further north, together with equally large consignments from Lincolnshire and Ireland.

GOOD POINTS OF THE EPICURE

Of recent years Epicure is a variety largely grown in Ayrshire on account of its early maturity. It is certainly not a good-looking potato, as it has deep eyes and is irregular in form. It also leaves much to be desired in point of flavour, but the fact that it is ready for raising in from ten to twelve weeks after planting is much in its favour for early work. Having resided in this district I have seen much of the methods employed.

Seaweed is plentiful all along the Ayrshire coast, and this is mixed with farmyard manure together with artificials like sulphate of potash, mineral phosphates and bone meal. The mixture is not laid in the drills as is customary in the south of Scotland, but is spread all over the surface and ploughed in so as to equally benefit the whole of the ground. The work of preparing the ground is advanced as much as possible, so that when a good season of planting is obtained no time is lost. The rows are generally from 24 in. to 28 in. apart with 12 in. to 15 in. from set to set.

The seed tubers are placed in the chitting trays at the previous raising time and are usually the third-sized. The trays are made to hold a bushel of seed by placing two or three layers thick. The Ayrshire growers often plant a second crop as soon as the first is gathered. This second crop is usually grown for seed.

DON'T CLAMP DISEASED POTATOES

In the first place, I need hardly refer to the utter folly of trying to preserve in clamps potatoes which are slightly diseased. Whenever potatoes, or in fact any roots, are placed in bulk, a certain amount of heat is evolved, and this rise in temperature helps to increase the disease much more rapidly than would be the case if the potatoes were laid out on a cold floor and kept covered with straw or sacking.

Again, if potatoes are to keep satisfactorily in the open, they must be put together in a dry condition.

The first step in making a clamp is to excavate about six inches of surface soil, allowing a width of 4 or 5 feet, according to the size of the tubers, the greater width being necessary in the case of the larger tubers. Place a layer of dry straw or leaves on the bottom of this, and then begin to stack up the potatoes.

If the weather is dry, do not be in a hurry to earth or mould up, but instead place a layer of straw over the tubers, in the same way as thatch is laid on a rick. This is necessary for two reasons: first, because should a heavy shower of rain be experienced, the water will then run off; and secondly, because the tubers, unless required for seed, should never be exposed to sunlight. A free circulation of air is necessary, and this can be best secured by means of wheat straw, barley straw being too soft.

EARTHING UP THE CLAMP

After a week or so, by which time the surplus heat should have escaped, earthing-up may commence.

Do not place soil on the top or crown of the clamp yet, but leave this open for another week or two for still more heat to escape. Also, before finally covering with straw to a depth of six to eight inches, place an old drain-pipe, or wisp of straw, in the top or high up in the sides, to admit of a free circulation of air. Heather or peat moss provides an excellent covering for potatoes, as also does dried bracken, while for temporary use the dried haulm may be used.

If potatoes become badly heated in the clamp, they never sprout well in spring, and after the long,

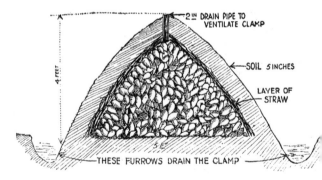

EARTHING UP THE CLAMP

thin and weak, tangled sprouts are removed, many of the tubers remain 'blind' when planted.

The opening of potato clamps must never be too long delayed in spring, otherwise the tubers soon begin to sprout, with the result that the growths become very long, and the whole contents of the heap become matted together. Under no conditions open a clamp during frosty weather. Another point is to select a dry day for bagging up the tubers, whether required for cooking or for seed, afterwards storing the bags in a cool place. The nearer the temperature is to 45°F the better.

The trays are then taken to the storing house and placed one on top of the other, and in some houses high piles representing some thousands of boxes are to be seen. Frost is carefully guarded against during the winter months, and when a few weeks near to planting time the temperature is raised in order to promote sprouting, when put in the ground each tuber will be furnished with several sprouts about an inch in length.

SPROUTING BOX TIP

To those who wish to make a reliable and strong sprouting box the following measurements will prove useful: Length of box, 2 ft; width, 1 ft; and height, 7 in. The size of the wood used should be: Side and bottom pieces, 3 by ⅜ in.; for the end pieces, 3 by ½ in.; and for the corner pieces, 1¼ in. square. The handle is made of material 1¼ in. square and is inserted in holes bored in the end pieces and kept in place by a nail driven in each end. The bottom pieces do not touch each other, a small space being left for ventilation. Many different types of boxes may be used, costing anything from 6d. to 1s. each.

SEED SPROUTING BOX OR CHITTING TRAY

Chapter 8

HINTS ABOUT GRADING
AND PACKING

We are often told that potatoes should follow this or that crop, as, for example, winter greens. On ordinary arable farms potatoes are an excellent cleaning crop, and I much prefer to take a crop of potatoes after a clover ley rather than to sow wheat, the wheat being made to follow the potatoes, in which case there is no loss of season and a clean seed-bed can be relied upon.

On many potato-growing farms there is nothing to make a rotation of, and thus we find that potatoes are grown year after year in the same soil. While I favour a rotation for many reasons, and especially where disease and insect pests are troublesome, potato-sick soil or even 'blight' is very little heard of on the Ayrshire coast, and it is nothing unusual to hear of potatoes being grown in the same field for fifty or sixty years without a break. Rye-grass or rape, however, is often ploughed in as a green manure crop.

In gardens potatoes follow cabbages, peas and beans, and are succeeded by autumn cabbages, onions, winter spinach, late lettuces, turnips and celery. When potatoes are intercropped with other plants, such as greens, mangels, etc., the place of such crop should be changed by shifting the potatoes a couple of feet or so.

USE OF MACHINERY

Machinery has come into prominence of late years in connection with potato-growing. The potato planter is of considerable service as an economiser of labour, but to ensure successful planting the tubers should be of fairly even size. The potato digger, of which there are many types, is also a great boon to growers. Sufficient gatherers in the form of women and boys are required to keep the digger moving over the ground, and if the gathering is well organised the horses will not lose any time. The digger does excellent work in light or loamy soil, and the great advantage it possesses over hand-forking is that very few tubers are damaged.

Early potato planting is all done by hand, and the raising by forks, as the tines of the horse machine would soon bruise the tender skins of the early crop and cause discolouring.

VALUE OF A GRADING MACHINE

The grading machine is indispensable for sorting or grading the main crop, and no potato grower or community of small growers should be without one. Small circular or the larger screening riddles are useful for small growers, but in no way compare with the rotary machines. Very early potatoes require no grading as they are sold as 'off the ground', and the small tubers are appreciated just as much as the larger ones.

Many growers prefer the potato plough to the digger, and it is, of course, a much cheaper implement. It does its work well and with little cutting or bruising. With a pair of horses and active gatherers

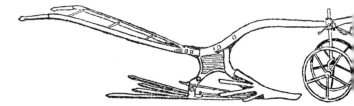

CONVERTIBLE POTATO RAISER
Admirably adapted for the small grower

from three to four acres may be raised in a day. Moreover, breasts and shares may be substituted for the raisers when the implement is changed into a serviceable ridging plough.

WHEN YOU PACK

The packing of potatoes requires care. Where crops are to be marketed direct from the field after raising, as is usually the case with most early and second early crops, it is preferable to grade, weigh and pack them on the ground. Apart from economy in labour the tubers are less damaged and shaken, a matter of no small importance, as the skins of early potatoes rub off so easily.

Potatoes should be graded into 'ware' or 'firsts', 'seconds' or seed, and thirds 'chats'. I find it much the best plan to sort the tubers into these sizes as they are gathered up after the fork, plough or digger.

In small cultivations where a potato sorter is not in use it is a good plan to collect the ware first, the seed size next and lastly the chats, together with any damaged or diseased potatoes that may remain.

It is never a wise plan to raise more potatoes than can be cleared up by the end of the day.

WHEN YOU WEIGH

In weighing potatoes a machine with a wooden platform, fitted with handles on either side, after the style of the wheelbarrow but without legs, is to be preferred to the tripod with scoop and spring balance. One great advantage of the former is that it can be carried close to the pickers and so save a lot of carrying.

These machines will support a large barrel or sack comfortably. The empties, whether hampers, barrels or sacks, must first be weighed, together with any packing material that may be necessary. It is a good plan to weigh a number of the packages to start with, putting the weight on the label for reference; this greatly facilitates weighing when the potatoes are being brought forward in large numbers.

There can be no greater waste of time where large consignments of early potatoes are to be dealt with than that of carting them to the store, to be again handled for the purpose of grading and weighing.

For very early potatoes bushel baskets are preferable, and later barrels of various sizes.

WHEN TO USE BAGS

Bags should only be used for the mid-season and late crops, as, having matured, the skins do not rub and bruise so readily. In the old days bags could be purchased for less than 2*d.* each, but at the time of writing 5*d.* to 6*d.* is nearer the price.

Provided that grading has been carefully carried out, there is little difficulty about packing. The mouth of the bag may be securely tied with twine, but should the bag just hold 1 cwt without leaving enough top to gather in the hand for tying, it must be stitched up by means of a packing needle.

Finally attach a label, on which is written the destination, grade and weight. Use a distinct coloured label for each variety if possible. I find this of great assistance where bags of seed are placed in store.

With barrels a little more care is necessary, as dried potato haulm, bracken or other material must be placed in the bottom before the 'empty' is weighed. Upon no consideration must any package be topped up with selected specimens, as this would amount to so much deception. A little packing material is placed in the top of the barrel and secured either by basket-work lids, or by cords fixed round the rims of the barrel for the purpose.

A bushel of potatoes, washed, weighs about 56 lb, and about 60 lb unwashed.

Chapter 9

DISEASES AND PESTS

We may now pass on to consider the diseases and insect pests which prove harmful to the potato crop. The weaker the constitution of any plant, the more liable it is to be attacked by pests of all kinds, and in the potato we have a plant the constitution of which has been much weakened by high or intensive cultivation.

Diseased potatoes are known to both the cultivator and the housewife. The outer skin is generally disfigured by the disease, although in some cases little external indication can be observed, and it is not until the tuber is cut through with a knife that the trouble is detected.

As a commercial grower one may be inclined to wonder whether the cost and trouble of spraying the crop repays the grower, as in some seasons disease does little or no harm, while in others very considerable havoc is wrought. Now that potatoes are so badly required, it is the duty of all, wherever possible, to take every precaution and to do all in their power to prevent either disease or insects from lessening the yield.

THE MOST SERIOUS DISEASE

'The' potato disease (known as *Phytophthora infestans*) is the most serious of all as regards its inroads into the nation's supply. The first and even the second early varieties, if planted in the proper season and raised early, rarely become attacked, as the spores of the disease are not then in evidence. It is during the damp, warm or sultry days of July that the spores of the disease develop and spread with such rapidity.

Millions of spores fall to the ground from the leaves and are washed into the ground, and if conditions are favourable to their germination will soon infest young tubers which are forming near to the surface. The first appearance of the disease is readily detected by the presence of light-brownish spots on the leaves, which gradually become darker. The fruiting branches of the fungus meanwhile form a delicate white mould or mildew.

The thread or 'root'-like body of the fungus, known as *Mycelium*, is supposed to pass down diseased stems into the young potatoes, and should the season be wet and the temperature what is known as close or muggy the mycelium contained in the potato continues to grow. This shortly causes brown spots to appear, resulting sooner or later in the rotting or decay of the tuber.

If, on the other hand, the infected potatoes are kept dry, the mycelium embedded in their flesh may remain dormant until the following spring. It will then become active and very soon infest the new crop, and finally appear in the fruiting condition on the leaves, as already alluded to, the fruiting bodies finding their way out through the breathing pores or stomata.

Growers and seedsmen have been eager to introduce a variety perfectly immune to potato disease, and have even tried crossing with the two hardy

British species of solanum that grow by the roadside, namely Bitter-sweet (*Solanum dulcanum*) and Black Solanum (*Solanum nigrum*), but the results were unsuccessful. The grafting of the potato on the tomato has also been tried, but in no case have the varieties proved immune. There is still, however, a possibility that just as rust-proof wheats have been evolved by judicious crossing, so may a perfect disease-resisting potato be finally produced.

SHOULD YOU BUY OR MAKE?

I first commenced spraying experiments twenty years ago, and know from experience that, taking one year with another, it pays to spray. Although Bordeaux mixture* is recommended in dealing with potato disease, I would advocate the use of one or other of the proprietary articles which will mostly become soluble immediately they are placed in water. Bordeaux mixture is composed of sulphate of copper and freshly burnt lime (quicklime), but in my opinion

---

* Bordeaux mixture is a traditional fungicide but no longer recommended as it is technically banned in the UK (except for very specific purposes) and the high level of copper it contains can be an environmental pollutant.

it is better to give a little more for the ready prepared materials, with which full directions as to use are given. Another reason why I advocate the prepared powder, is that unless the home-made mixture is used up within a day or two, there is risk of destroying the foliage due to excessive acidity. The mixture must be alkaline enough to neutralise its acidity.

The amount of spray fluid required per acre is usually from 100 to 150 gallons, but I find that in field application where a horse machine is used this quantity is often exceeded in cases where the crop is heavy and the horse moves slowly, and where there is a deal of short turns. The cost will average about 12s. per acre at the present-time rates. In small gardens or allotments a knapsack sprayer or spraying syringe will perform the work quite successfully.

Personally I always give three sprayings, one at the end of June, followed by two more at intervals of a fortnight.

ABOUT DRY SPRAYING

I have also tried dry spraying, which consists of distributing the powder of copper salts in a fine state of division by blowing it over the damp foliage. Small hand machines are made for the purpose, but I must say that I do not find the process so convenient as wet spraying; also the operation must be very carefully performed. Spray for preference in the evening, when the foliage is damp from dew; never wet- or dry-spray when rain is near at hand.

Do not wait until the crop is diseased before commencing to spray, remembering that the act of spraying is a preventive and not a curative of the trouble.

Diseased potatoes left in the soil and even slightly diseased 'sets' are a source of infection for subsequent crops. A proper rotation must be observed, and all haulm burnt as soon as it can be gathered together.

BLACK LEG OR STEM ROT

This disease is more prevalent on the Continent than in this country, and is caused by a germ called *Bacillus phytophthorus*. The symptoms of the disease are as follows. The leaves wilt and turn yellow, and finally become shrivelled and die from below upwards. Upon examination of the underground stem, the surface is found to be more or less covered with brownish stains. This discoloration gradually spreads upwards, the stem finally becoming black and rotten.

Plants with this disease are usually found growing amongst perfectly healthy ones, but the adjoining plants are nevertheless liable to become affected, especially during hot, damp days in June and July. As a preventative it is advised not to cut the sets; also to be careful in their selection. Avoid a too liberal use of lime or of strong nitrogenous manures.

SCAB IN POTATOES

Scab in potatoes is a common form of disease, but there are several sorts of scab, some more or less harmless, and others of a very serious character, causing widespread damage to the crop. It is quite easy to imagine how the skin of a delicate tuber like the potato becomes scratched in gritty soils, and as the tuber increases in size the abrasion must of necessity enlarge and form into a scab.

The principal forms of scab are wart disease or black scab, due to a fungus known as *Synchytrium endobioticum*, and corky scab, due to *Spongospora scabies*, while apart from scab due to mechanical injury there is still another form due to the fungus *Oospora scabies*, and still another caused by millipedes. The *Oospora* scab of potatoes is most common, the fungus attacking the tubers in their young state and causing scattered rough blotches to form on the surface.

This form of scab is recognised as distinct from the other forms by the presence of the parasite which makes its appearance on wounded potatoes as a delicate greyish bloom. Fortunately the injury is confined to the skin of the tubers, the flesh remaining quite wholesome. If 'scab-bed' seed is used for planting the resulting crop is almost certain to be affected. To remedy this it is advisable to immerse the tubers for two hours in a solution consisting of half a pint of commercial formalin* mixed with eighteen gallons of water, afterwards spreading the potatoes out to dry. It is said that lime favours the development of the fungus in the soil, and the same remarks apply to stable manure and night soil. Acid manures should be applied to soils infected with scab.

---

* Formalin (embalming fluid) should never be used to disinfect potatoes.

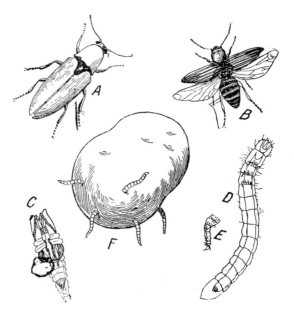

WIRE WORMS
(ELATERIDÆ)

A & B Striped click beetle (*Agriotes lineatus*). C Pupa.
D Larva or wire-worm. E Jointed leg of larva.
F Wire-worms attacking potatoes.

FALSE WIRE-WORMS

I have seen large numbers of tubers badly attacked by millipedes, which are often known as false wire-worms. They often cause numerous shallow cavities in the flesh of the potatoes, each wound becoming surrounded by corky tissue, and presenting a scabbed appearance. The injury may also develop into larger and deeper cavities, having no resemblance to scab. These are, however, often associated with attacks by slugs and soil insects. The true wire-worms, which are the tough-skinned larvæ of the click beetle, also attack the tubers and impair their appearance.

Wart disease or black scab in potatoes attacks the tubers, giving rise to ugly abnormal growths like miniature cauliflowers, except that they are dark in colour. In some instances these warts may appear at the surface of the soil, and can sometimes be detected at the base of the stem as yellowish-green masses. The disease is most prevalent in potato-sick soils, or where the crop is grown in short rotations.*

* Although now controlled, Potato Wart Disease is a notifiable disease that should be reported to Defra.

INFECTED LAND

Infected land may be rendered unfit for potato-growing for six or even more years, and even then those varieties of potatoes should only be planted that are known to resist the disease. Diseased tubers contain numberless disease spores which when mature are capable of infecting healthy potatoes in the following season. These spores may lie dormant in the soil for several years without losing their power of infection. The planting of even one infected tuber might be the means of establishing the disease on a holding, as there are so many agencies by which the spores become dispersed.

While it is recommended that diseased potatoes should be fed to cattle or pigs, the tubers should always be well boiled before feeding, as if fed in a raw state the disease would be readily spread by the manure of the animals. For similar reasons the diseased haulm should always be burnt and not thrown on the manure heap, and this should always be done as soon as possible after the crop is lifted; otherwise the haulm is apt to decay and get worked into the soil. Samples of seed should always be carefully examined before planting; also should any diseased plants be observed in the crop these should be dug out, the tubers boiled, and the haulm destroyed to prevent the spread of the disease. It is only by preventing the development and spread of the disease that the trouble can be effectively dealt with: there is no other remedy.

LEAF CURL HAVOC

Among the early varieties of potatoes, and occasionally among the later crops, much havoc is wrought by potato leaf curl, which is readily detected by the stunted growth of the haulm, the small size of the leaflets, while very often the shoots do not even get above ground, as indicated by gaps in the rows.

Infection may arise through the presence of spores in the soil attacking the young sprouts, or the haulm may become affected by the hibernating mycelium passing directly from the tubers. In any case growth is arrested due to the circulation of water and food being checked by the upward growth of the fungus in the tissues of the haulm. As the mycelium increases in quantity the haulm becomes flabby and the leaves gradually lose their rigidity and curl. In raising the plant the tubers will be found undersized but firm and hard.

Where the foliage is infected the crop should be lifted as soon as possible. If this is done the seed may be quite good for planting, as it is not until the later stages that the tubers become affected. I have noticed that the disease is more prevalent in hot, dry, sandy soils, and particularly in seasons of drought. As in all other attacks of fungoid diseases, the foliage and stems should be burnt, as it is only by cleanliness in this way and in keeping the soil sweet that these troubles can be kept in check.

WINTER ROT

Winter rot or sprain of potatoes is a fungoid disease which attacks the tuber when in the ground, usually through the medium of wounds made by slugs, wire-worms, or by other agencies, or where the skin has been injured in lifting. Such tubers often remain unchanged in appearance, and are often planted under the impression that they are quite sound. After planting, the fungus becomes very active, the mycelium spreading quickly and destroying the young sprouts, while on raising the crop the seed will be found perfectly hard and unchanged. Should the tubers be stored before they are thoroughly dry the skin remains soft and is easily burst by the fungus, which forms small white warts on the surface, followed by collapse and the wrinkling of the part affected, thus allowing other fungi, bacteria, mites, etc., to gain an easy entrance, with the result that the flesh of the tuber is quickly reduced to a bad-smelling pulp. If the haulm dies down gradually the tubers are less liable to attack.

Probably the best preventative of winter rot is to dry the tubers very thoroughly before storing. This is too often neglected, and there is no greater mistake than that of rushing potatoes together into a heap directly they come off the ground. Powdered sulphur, if sprinkled over the tubers at the rate of 2 lb per ton, is known to destroy the fungus, and will also keep in check woodlice, mites and other pests which are often responsible for conveying the spores of the disease from one tuber to another. The fungus spreads very rapidly when clamps are closed down too early, and for this reason I have always advocated plenty of ventilation in the clamps, so long as there is no risk of frost.

Chapter 10

FEEDING POTATOES TO LIVE STOCK

We have all seen the time when potatoes as well as wheat could be more profitably fed to stock than sold in the market at unremunerative prices.

There is little reliable data pertaining to the value of potatoes for stock-feeding as compared with other root crops, but most farmers have realised that the crop requires very careful feeding. For horses, potatoes excel all other roots in value, and especially for animals performing heavy work, but of a slow nature. The tubers should be cooked and served judiciously, so as to avoid too much relaxation of the bowels. Needless to add, a portion of the corn would be withheld and the quantity of water materially curtailed.

Potatoes have also been fed with advantage to horses in their raw state, sliced with chaff, but where it has been convenient to boil or steam them the benefit has been greater. The proportion of potatoes in the ration is usually accepted as 1 lb potatoes to 2½ lb of the other ingredients. It has been claimed that 15 lb of potatoes yield as much nourishment as 4½ lb of oats, and that 3 bushels of potatoes are equal to 1 cwt of hay.

Potatoes, when plentiful and cheap, have been freely used in the rations for dairy cows in this country. The tubers are cleaned and steamed or boiled, and served whole, while warm, with chopped hay or straw. From two to three gallons is a fair daily allowance for an average Shorthorn cow in full profit. I have known some farmers who pulp the raw tubers, in which case the starch of the potato is less digestible.

COOK THE POTATOES

All those who have tried feeding the tubers, both raw and cooked, speak in favour of cooking, as the potatoes are then twice as nutritious as any other roots. A few cooked potatoes mixed in hay chaff make an excellent first solid food for calves after they have attained the age of from six to eight weeks. If any undue looseness or scouring is noticed then the quantity of potatoes must be gradually reduced.

For strong fattening steers and heifers something rather more bulky than potatoes is required, and, for the purpose of fattening, swedes and mangels are preferable and admit of being fed in larger quantities.

PROFITABLE FOR PIGS

Potatoes are fed more profitably to pigs than to any other class of stock. There has been a lot of discussion as to the advisability of feeding potatoes raw or cooked to pigs, but I have no hesitation in saying that when it comes to finishing off either porkers or bacon hogs potatoes are of little use unless boiled and mashed along with meal.

FLAVOUR IN POTATOES

What is commonly regarded as flavour in potatoes is dry mealiness or starchiness, resembling flour, with which is associated a slight taste of salt. While there are varieties of potatoes which give flesh that is always close and soapy, there are very many which, grown in suitable soil, provide this dry mealy flesh, and such tubers always command admiration. But even with these much depends upon soil, and if a soil be deficient in lime or phosphates, then the tubers, even of the best varieties, are poor eating, however cooked. The best tubers I have ever tasted came off chalk soil.

COOKING OF POTATOES

Potatoes do not all cook alike, and there can be little doubt that some varieties are spoiled in the cooking. For many years the writer had occasion to test the cooking qualities of potatoes, and the different treatment required by certain varieties was most striking. The potato is certainly not treated fairly when fried, or disguised when cooked in other and similar ways. To realise the quality of a potato it must be boiled. The skin or rind of the potato contains a poisonous substance known as *solanine*, which is destroyed or dissipated when the potatoes are boiled or steamed.

In large establishments the skins are now rubbed off by friction with some revolving and dentated plate or surface, the eyes being removed or scooped out afterwards. In the ordinary peeling of potatoes too thick a rind is usually removed; also there is no greater mistake than that of allowing the peeled and cut tubers to soak in cold water before cooking, as by doing so much of the soluble food matter is lost. For a like reason the tubers should never be allowed to start boiling in cold water, as this is a common cause of waxiness.

It is estimated that the potato is made up approximately as follows: skin 2.5 per cent, inner layer next to skin 8.5 per cent, and flesh 89 per cent. The inner layer and the flesh comprise the edible portion, which contains about 75 per cent of water, so that only about 25 per cent is of direct value as food, and the richest part of the potato is that next to the skin. It is easy therefore to realise the great waste incurred by the thick peeling of potatoes, and which is of course more often practised where the tubers are deep-eyed, the loss in some cases amounting to as much as 20 per cent of the whole tuber. Not only do these surface layers, which are wasted, contain a larger percentage of solids than the remainder, but the subsequent boiling liberates soluble ingredients of the potato, while the surface of the potato breaks down into the water and is thrown away.

THE CORRECT METHOD

The correct method of cooking the potato is to peel off the skin as thinly as possible, and immediately immerse the tubers in boiling water in an iron saucepan, meanwhile adding some salt. Keep the water boiling steadily, neither too fast nor too slow. When the tubers are rather more than half done, pour off all but just enough water to cover the bottom of the pan, allowing the pan to stand near the fire with the lid slightly tilted to liberate the steam, but not near enough to burn. If the potatoes cannot be consumed at once, place a clean white cloth over them to prevent them becoming sodden with steam, thereby losing their flavour.

A pared potato put into cold water and boiled will lose 15.8 per cent of its flesh-forming matter or protein, 18.8 per cent of its ash or mineral matter, and 3 per cent of its carbohydrates or starch. If, after paring, the potato is plunged at once into boiling water and boiled it loses 8.2 per cent of its flesh-formers, 18 per cent of its ash, and only about 0.2 per cent of its starch. In the case of a potato boiled in its jacket, on the other hand, the loss is only 1 per cent of flesh-formers, 3 per cent of ash, and practically none of starch.

Therefore from a nutritive and economic point of view, potatoes should be cooked in their 'jackets'. By so doing there is practically no waste of food material, and further the flavour of many varieties is considerably better than when peeled. To cook potatoes in their jackets, first well wash them in cold water, after first cutting out any damaged eyes or fractures. To prevent potatoes boiled or steamed in their jackets from becoming 'stodgy' a cut should be made in each end of the tuber. Then place in a saucepan with sufficient cold water to nearly cover them, and as soon as the water boils add a little more cold water at intervals. A little salt should be added with each supply of water. Test with a fork to see if they have boiled through, and if so pour off the water, and hold the saucepan over the fire to enable the moisture to evaporate.

If they cannot be served at once, place in a thick white cloth in the oven until required.

WHEN YOU BAKE THEM

Baked potatoes are much relished by most people, and in this form they are very nourishing. Select large tubers of varieties like Great Scot and Arran Chief. Wash the skins well and prick them or cut them before baking. Place them in a moderately warm oven, turning the tubers at intervals. They will take from one and a half to two hours to cook properly and should be served in napkins. Slow cooking is necessary in the baking of potatoes, so that the skin does not 'bake on' to the 'flesh' and so cause loss.

Many people prefer their potatoes cooked by steam, in which case a proper potato steamer should be procured and the tubers, either peeled or with their jackets on, placed in the drainer with water beneath. The water should be poured off directly the tubers are cooked.

INDEX